I Speak to All
Just So

I Speak to All Just So

Galen Pearl

STILL CREEK PRESS
PORTLAND, OREGON

I Speak to All Just So
Sill Creek Press, Portland, OR

© 2022 by Galen Pearl

Book design by Vinnie Kinsella, Paper Chain Book Publishing Services (paperchainbps.com)

ISBN: 978-0-9858462-3-7
eISBN: 978-0-9858462-4-4

In the deep dark of mystery
Where we all came from
and still are
In the vast silence
humming
We've forgotten
This is a book of remembering who we are

Contents

An elegant journal was gifted to me by a friend who didn't know that I no longer kept a journal, that indeed, all my journals spanning decades had been offered to the fire in a great conflagration of liberation. So the gifted journal sat, waiting patiently, until one day I picked it up and wrote a prayer in it. I'm not really a praying person, or rather I am, but not in the traditional sense. Yet the journal invited sacred dialogue, so I wrote a prayer and waited. I don't remember how I knew what to do next, but the pen found its way to my non-dominant left hand, and a response to the prayer was written.

By whom? I do not know. I suppose by the one to whom the prayer was prayed. And who was that? Again, I do not know. I prayed when my need spoke to the Universe, which in my prayers I addressed by various names. The name matters not. My prayers were answered from that place within me that is beyond me, beyond names.

Thus began a practice that continued for several years. After writing a prayer I listened, and wrote the words I heard. The hearing and the writing occurred simultaneously, without time to consider or edit before the words were on the page. Sometimes I was surprised by the content of the answers, or by the way in which they were phrased. I didn't understand it, but I learned to trust the process, to receive with humble gratitude the encouragement, correction, and assurance given with such unfailing, exquisite love.

And then, with one last response, the practice ended. At first perplexed and a little saddened, I came to understand that there was no longer a need to separate from Oneness to have a sacred dialogue. The prayers and responses merged into wordless guidance, ever present and available.

I hesitated to include a description of how this book was written, because it's easy to get distracted by a particular technique, to mistake the process for the message. As the title of the book suggests, the message is universal, broadcast eternally on all frequencies of existence. The message is the vibration of life itself. *How* we hear it is unimportant. *That* we hear it is inevitable. So listen. Listen within, listen with every cell of your being to the song the universe sings in your soul. You will recognize its vibration, resonating in perfect harmony with your heart. Awaken to the memory of who you are and know that you are unimaginably loved.

> *There are no words in Oneness*
> *Words create two*
> *When I speak*
> *I speak to God*
> *Who else is there?*

PRAYERS AND RESPONSES

I yield this year to you
Create in me a supple heart
Open to your guidance
Desiring to serve
Willing to be wounded
Abiding in your loving embrace
Shielded by your wings
Shining with your light
Spreading your joy
Living for you
I yield this year to you

Beloved, I shelter you and love you
I lift you up to shine my light
You have had a big task and you have done well
Much has been healed
You will see all someday
Now give yourself to me
You are a holy offering
I bless you and keep you
You are my beloved child
Trust me and follow me
You will see and do more than you can possibly imagine
Smile
All is well

On this the day of my birth
I am thankful
I am thankful for my life
For the parents who bore me and raised me
For the abundance you have entrusted to me
For the lessons you have offered me
For the love you have shown me
For the healing you have blessed me with
For the children you have treasured with me
For all that has been and will be and is now
I am thankful

Child of my heart
Daughter of my soul
You are treasured and beloved
On this day and all days
You are celebrated in heaven
The angels sing your name
It is the place of God
You are joy my joy
You are sweet honey
Go forth in love
Embraced by angels
Held in the hands of the One
Who loves you
Now and forever

Here I am
To hear your call
To do my best
Even though I don't feel qualified
I trust your guidance
Your qualifications fill me
Instruct me
Guide me
Inspire me
I yield to your wisdom
I will follow where you lead
I will not fear
You will show me the way
You will guide my steps
You will not let me fall
Your way is perfect
I yield to you

Child of my heart
I will not let you fall
I will teach you my ways
I will cover you with my wings
You are safe and loved
Do not fear the darkness
Trust the lighted path
Be humble and listen
Be patient and still
You will hear my words on butterfly wings
The breeze will whisper
The trees will sing
Be still and give me your attention
I am here with you always

Thank you
Thank you for my life
Thank you for the abundant blessings you have
    given me
I live in safety
I have a home
I am not hungry
I can provide for my children
I have good health
And good friends
You have led me through some dark times
Into the light of joy
You have lifted me up
And blessed me
I praise you in gratitude

Live in joy, beloved child
Dance in the light
Shine your spirit bright
Light the way for others
Give what you have been given
Your way will be made manifest
Follow your breath
I breathe you to heaven

What have you brought to us
A wondrous mystery
A gift of new life
An opportunity to grow in faith
An opportunity to yield
I do yield
I yield to your perfect plan
To your infinite wisdom
To your abounding love
I sink into your embrace
I sigh in trust
I am safe
In you

Ah child
You know I am here
I will not leave you
I will not forsake you
You are indeed safe
In the refuge under my wings
Struggle not
Your way is set
Your path made straight
I guide your steps
You will not fall
Open your heart
To all the love
That's all there is
It is beautiful

l struggle
l sink in despair
l hide in shame
l seethe in anger
l whine in self pity
Why do l do this harm to myself
Please help me stop
Please help me not hurt those l love
Please help me break through these blocks
Please help me not repeat what hurt me
Use me to bring forgiveness
And grace
Cleanse my spirit of everything that is not your
    shining love
Help me yield completely
To you

My beloved
Everything is a gift
Everything is a miracle
A door of opportunity
To walk into the garden
Come walk with me
Do not listen to the others
Idle chatter
Pay it no mind
Here is paradise
What else is there to choose
Come with me
Into the garden
Behold
It is here
Come
Take my hand
Come

Wonder of miracles
I feel the earth shift
Clean water pours in
The beginnings of return to peace
The waters calm
Reflecting faith
It is as it is
And as it is
Is how it should be
Because all is yours
And perfect

Beloved, be a mirror
Look at yourself and remember
There but for my grace...
Yes you know it's true
I embrace you with the truth
It will make you free
Beloved, be a window
Clear and spotless
Letting the light shine through
In perfect love and harmony
Be an open window
Allowing pure breath
The breath of life
To flow
Allowing the music of the spheres
The harmony of angels
To breathe into every life

Keeper of my soul
Home of my heart
Hear me now
Hear my prayer
I don't know what is happening
I call upon you
Guide me through this
I want only to follow you
Shine your light of love
Upon my fear
Guard my thoughts and words
And keep them holy
Hear my prayer
I ask for miracles

Miracles are yours my loved one
They always are
In infinite number
They are yours
You have but only to open your eyes
And see them
Trust me
    without hesitation
    without doubt
Rejoice in my perfection
    which is your own
Fear not
For there is nothing to fear
There is only love
Love them as I love you
Be at peace
All is well

Giver of peace
Shepherd of my soul
Teacher, guide, and friend
My mind tosses like the waves once calmed
I doubt
   and fear
Worry lines my brow
Distress crushes my spirit
I sink in anxiety
Reach out your hand to me
Lift me from the dark water
Breathe faith into my spirit
Quiet the tempest in my heart
Help me follow you

Beloved lamb
My arms are here
To lift you up
Do not be afraid
There is nowhere you can go
Away from the safety of my embrace
My love is pure and strong
You are safe
And so are they
Release everything to me
I will restore you
My smile will warm your spirit
My cloak is soft and clean
Nestle close and rest
Turn you face to me
And only me
That is enough
That is everything

You are giving me a great opportunity this year
A year of old memories surfacing to be healed
A year of transition
Letting go of who I was
To become who I will be
A year of surprises
    to teach me...what?
I am asking for miracles
Miracles of healing what is past
Miracles of becoming who you want me to be
Miracles of acceptance and wisdom and joy
To welcome what is new

Babe in my arms
In my heart
Babe birthed from my love
From nowhere else
I am showering you with miracles
An abundance of miracles
Let go and trust me
Wary one
Weary one
Just stop
Receive the bounty
Do not doubt
Yield to me
Yield, beloved
Yield

Thank you for my blessings
You bless me with abundance
I lack for nothing
You fill me with your teaching
    of love
    of patience
    of mercy
    of willingness
    of courage
    of trust
    of forgiveness
    of compassion
    of faith
You fill me with yearning
To love you all my days with every breath
To sing your glory in every moment
To wait for you knowing you will come
Knowing you are here

Precious lamb
You are mine
You do well
I am pleased
What joy there is in obedience to me
    to my way
    the way home
Where we are one as we have been
    and ever are
Take heart dear one
Have courage
Your race is almost done
Rest in me
In peace and joy

God of birth and death
I thank you for the precious gift of life
From this moment on
For as many moments as I have left in this lifetime
Let me use each moment
    to spread your love
    to shine your light
    to create sacred space
    to honor truth
    to follow your teaching
    to pray without ceasing
    to open completely
    to yield myself
      give myself
        surrender myself
    to dissolve and disappear into the ocean of you
Until everything is gone and words are no more

Come to me
Little one
Brave one
Beloved
This is all for you
This gift
My gift to you
To bring you home
Love your life
Precious one
The breath I breathe into you
Is me

Goddess of infinite mercy
Thank you for the abundance you have bestowed
on me
Thank you for yesterday
A day I will remember always
Thank you for my children
my greatest honor
my greatest wealth
my greatest gift
Thank you for humbling me by reminding me of
what matters
Thank you for miracles

Dear one
I send my love through others
Perfect vessels
I am giving you the opportunity
To see through the illusion
To see the truth
Let everything else fall away
Live in the light
Live the miracle

My life clatters with to do lists too long
Scatters with things I want to do
So many things
My mind is filled with mind kittens
Things desired become ought-tos
    and need-tos
    and have-tos
    and shoulds
Joy drains
Peace roils
Stillness shatters
Control chokes yield
Dread deadens trust
Fear reaches tentacles into faith
Have mercy on me
Pour your nectar of compassion to cool my fevered
    soul
Please help me
I need you

Oh child
Just stop
Take a breath
My breath
Let me breathe for you
You need but ask
That's all
Take my hand and follow me
To still waters and green pastures
Seek ye first...and only...
Me
Your willingness is all it takes to yield
Then your job is done
The rest is mine
So look...here
Keep your eyes on me
Go forth in joy and peace
Forever

Merciful one
Please help me
My heart is churned up
The water is murky
I cannot see
Loved ones are in danger
Where is my path
What would you have me do
Please lead me and guide me
Show me the way I should go
Please protect them
Hold them in your hands
Send your angels to embrace them
Surround them with the light of your love
Heal their hearts and keep them safe

Dear child
Do you not know
That all are in my hands
I hold them all and you
You know not their paths
It is not yours to know
Yours is to have faith
Only that
Pray for faith
And it will be yours
All is well
Believe
Breathe
Be still...and know

Beloved
I long to live in your constant embrace
Following your path
Obeying your teaching
Living in holy rapture
My eyes seeing only your light
My ears hearing only your voice
My tongue drinking only your nectar
My nose smelling only your fragrance
My skin feeling only your touch
Accept me as your own
Grant my prayer to be yours and yours alone
Awaken within me unquenchable divine fire
That will burn forever
Shining as the sun
Dispelling the darkness
Hear my prayer

My beloved child
I welcome you on this path
You are returning home
Where you belong
I hear your prayer
I know what is in your heart
You are home already
Safe in my arms
Awaken child
Open your eyes and see
Behold
It is as it is

I seek you with all my heart
But my mind is confused
So many claims
So many words
So many who "know"
This way is the one way
No that one
A mistake seems costly
So I listen for you in the silence
I wait for you all day long
Teach me your way
Lead me on your path
Guide my steps
Have mercy on me
Show me the way
Give me wisdom to see it
And courage to follow it
Protect me under your wings
Thanks be to you forever

You get distracted like a child at Christmas
All is window dressing
The ten thousand things
Follow the eternal Dao
Nameless
Formless
Found in the silence of your soul
The way of no way
All else is fear and separation
An illusion of the world you have created
Rest and be still
Know that we are one
And all is well
Love of my heart
Be at peace
In me

There is so much suffering
I think I can't bear it
My heart explodes with grief
My lungs drown in sorrow
I look around my world at so much pain
How can this be enlightening
How can there be any basic goodness in this much
    muck
It is so raw a tiny touch burns like the flames of hell
Everywhere
Everywhere
Where is peace
Where are *you*

I am here
In the layers deep inside
Come closer
Walk into the fire
    into the storm
        into the pit
Right into the jaws of hell
And there you will see
It was all nothing
Just a dream
Trust when you cannot trust
That is faith
My gift to you because you are mine
Take heart
Walk into the fire
It will burn you to life

I suffer in shame
The shame is so deep and horrible
I'm so ashamed of who I was
So desperate for love, for relief from pain
Willing to turn a blind eye to truth
I was so lost, so lost, so lost
Now I'm found, but the shame lingers
There was shame that wasn't mine
But this shame is mine
Isn't it?
I don't even know
How can I forgive this
Please help me
I need a miracle
I'm afraid
It hurts
Lead me to truth
I am ready

Beloved child
When you open to love
The world comes in
Love heals
All that is ugly will be purified
Let me in
The spirit sees and cleans
Do not resist
Do not fear
You are home
Now and always
Miracles abound
No harm will come to you
Yield to me
Everything

Another year comes to an end
A big year—full of changes and surprises
A year of learning to trust you more
    of yielding more
    of loving more
Friends of different faiths
Each telling me to follow their way
It gets so confusing when it is really so simple
It's only you I want
I want to love you and follow you
I want to yield myself to you
    to die to you
    to live in you
Every moment with every breath
I want to live your promise
    to manifest your love
    to release anything I put in the way of union
        with you
I am here
Merciful one, thank you for loving me
For showering me with your abundant blessings

Lamb of love
You are mine
Now and forever
Go forward into the new year
Rejoicing
With a song in your heart
Angels sing with you
As they carry you where there is no harm
Ever safe
Ever loved
Ever mine
Fret not over concerns for others
All are in my care
Trust me
The darkness cannot last
It gives way before the light of truth
Rejoice now and forevermore
You are home

You are my home
My mind wanders here and there
But my heart rests always in your love
How can I serve you
What would you have me do
Where would you have me go
What would you have me say, and to whom

Greetings, my child
I delight in your love
Serve me with your breath
  with your sight
  with your peace
Serve me by teaching others what you know
Help them remove the blinders from their eyes
Bless them with light
Lead them by following me
Serve with humility
Strong in faith
Bathed in light
Sheltered in love
Know that all is well
Be steady
Open
Still
Listen
You will know

I come to you
To offer all I am
All I have
All I can
To you
I forget sometimes
That I am home
That I am with you
Always
I forget that there is no I
That all I am
All I have
All I can
Is but a dream
All I have to offer
Is a dream
From which I would awaken
Help me to wake up
And know that there is nothing to know
There is only you
There is only....

Child of Light
Be at peace
Bathed in rainbows
Take my hand
And let all else fall away
Here is everything you seek
Breathe it in
Fear not
Be at peace
Let it go
Believe in…nothing
The great cloud from which stars are born
The beginning of heaven and earth
The place where we are…not
Because there is no we
The great emptiness
Come in and see
Hear the laughter in the silent energy
Come in and fall away

Light, Love, Joy, Peace
I forget and lose my way
I get caught up in tasks, in ambition, in ego
I worry about the things I do not know
I chafe at things that take up my time
I forget the only thing that matters
You
"Seek ye first…"
Sometimes I see you last
"Love God with all…"
Sometimes I love you with what's left
Today is a new day
I recommit myself to you
To you first
To you all
I place all else at your feet
In humble trust
I wait

Child of the ten thousand things
You scatter your pearls
In hope of deserving
No need
No want
No fear
Child of the beginning of heaven and earth
Rest in the mystery
Knowing nothing
Perfection
All else falls away
Illusion
Light shines everywhere
You are the light
You are light
Arise and shine

I read a story of faith
Faith so pure and powerful and infinite
Faith that yields completely
Surrenders fully
Holds nothing back
Forgives all
Fears nothing
I want faith like that
I want to pray without ceasing
I want my life, my very breath
To be a prayer
I want to be so filled with spirit
That there is nothing left of me
All that remains will be prayer
Teach me to pray
Lead me in faith

Beloved child
Listen
And I will teach you
Open your heart
Come to me
Give yourself to me
Remember who you are
Learn my way
Be one
Beloved

Over and over I drift away
I get busy, distracted, anxious, scattered
But you find me every time
With gentle patience you lead me home again
What love is this
That never grows weary
Never despairs
Never condemns
Worthiness becomes meaningless in the arms of
   grace
Thank you
Thank you
Thank you

You are mine
always
Precious
always
Embraced
always
Welcomed
always
Safe
always
Perfect
always
Loved
always

I come before you boldly
In bold thanksgiving
In bold asking
"Ask and you will receive"
So I'm asking
I'm asking for faith
I want faith bigger than a mustard seed
Faith that can move more than mountains
Faith that shines brighter than the sun
Faith that heals beyond miracles
Faith that fills me up until I dissolve
Until light and love are all that remain
Faith that transcends all problems,
    all limitations, all lack, all doubt
Faith that bows in humble gratitude
Bold faith
This I ask
This I ask

Then this you shall have
Faith in abundance
Faith beyond limits
You are blessed with faith
Fear not
You will see marvelous things
Beyond your understanding
Release your hold
And fly with the wings I will give you
Remember the angels
Everything is perfect
Faith I give to you
All I ask is your willingness to receive it
Even just your willingness to be willing
I will do the rest
Believe
Believe you are anointed with love
And all is well
Go in peace and in faith
I touch you
...now

I asked and you gave
The receiving is not always easy
I stumble in fear
But you lift me up as promised
I come to you in gratitude
With songs of thanksgiving
Seeing the blessings
Playing with angels
Resting in your embrace
Delighting in your presence
Goddess of Love
Hold me ever near
Next to your heart
In your heart
Always

Your delight is mine as well
The heavens sing with joy
Hope is born
Faith blossoms
Love abounds
Be at peace in the perfection
All is well
I love you, my precious child
You are my heart song
Light in eternity
Pure and everlasting
It is

Creator of the universe
Source of all
One, infinite, beyond, timeless
Bring me home
Teach me to meditate on you
   all day long
      and through the night
Teach my eyes to see only your light
My ears to hear only your song
My heart to fill with your love
Lead me beside still waters
Still waters that will fill my soul with peace
I grow weary with scattered effort
Fragmented unfocus fatigues me
Strengthen my resolve
Train me in your ways
Let me not be deterred or distracted
Help me
I am shaken and overwhelmed
My mind resists—why?
You are all I long for
Have mercy on me

I hear your cry my child
Fear not
The lilies toil not
Neither need you
No effort but willingness
Attend
Yield
Shine
There is nowhere to go
You are already home
Awake from your dream
The riches of heaven are yours
Rejoice with your brother
For you belong to me
And all is well
Peace I give to you
Receive it beloved
I say it is so
So be it

I ask and you give
Yet here I am again
    asking again
        in need again
I drift away again
Knowing that I do
Until I need your help again
    to come home
        to know that I am home
           to know I never left
Today I seek your word
A word to share
Open my ears again
    my heart again
        my soul again
Help me yield again
Most merciful wonder
    who never tires
        who always responds
           who loves me patiently
Thank you
Help me live my thanks again

Child
As many times
  hundreds
    thousands
      millions
        beyond count
As many times as you turn to me
I am here
As many times as you turn away
I am here
Each time you turn to me
Is cause for rejoicing
Each time you turn away
Is cause for rejoicing
Why is this?
Because you can never turn in any direction
I am not
Is that not cause for joy?
So turn as you like
Until you see that all turning is towards the light
Until you see there is no turning
Laugh with me my child
Fall into my arms again and again
There is nowhere else

Another year
Urgency, yearning, longing
Wanting you
Fearing I fall short
Frustrated with my scattered monkey mind
Lazy in my efforts
Hesitant, muddled, moving
Always moving
Help me still my mind, quiet my soul
Teach me to listen, to wait
To trust you, to turn to you, to yield to you
With every breath
Give me the insight to know what I hold back
And the courage to offer it to you
Wholly, joyfully
With relief and gratitude and love
Remove my fear and fill me with your light
    everlasting
Use me for the purpose you would have me serve
Purify my heart so that I will see you
And live with you forever

As you ask so shall it be
Wait is your word
Breathe it in and out until it becomes part of you
Wait for me
For I will surely come
Wait my child
For I will surely come

Waiting
Waiting
Engaged waiting
Distracted waiting
Impatient waiting
Arrogant waiting
Special waiting
Discouraged waiting
Hopeless waiting
Desperate waiting
Frightened waiting
Moments of peaceful waiting
    joyful expectancy
        quiet anticipation
Just moments
Teach me to wait
To wait for you
Only and always
To be ready
To be willing
To live in the waiting

My child
You have only touched the surface
Not even that
I gave you this word because you are ready
Trust me
It won't be easy but you are able
Now just be willing
Don't do what fear tells you to do
Wait
Wait with your whole self
Do not be led away
Do not fear
Give everything to me
Everything
Then you will have even more
Your heart's desire
Wait
Forever
Eternity is in this moment
Enter

I understand now
The miracle I'm asking for is not out there
It's in me
The change of heart I seek
Is my own
Grant me the serenity to accept the things I cannot
    change
And the courage to change the only thing I can
Myself
And even that change is at your hands, not mine
Thank you for giving me this lesson
For teaching me to rely only on you
    to wait only for you
    to trust only in you
    to rejoice in all things
The arrows turn to flowers
Transformed by your perfect love
Purify my spirit
Fill my senses with only you
Blessed in your arms
Safe under your wings

Peace be to you
and in you
and all around you
My peace I give to you
All is well
Rest in comfort
Secure in knowing
Removed from all conflict
Give thanks for everything
Because everything brings you closer to me
Be grateful and joyful
Everything is in my hands
Your safety is not of this world
So don't look for it there
Look at me
Only me
There is nothing else to see
Rest my child
I guard your sleep

I've been struggling to be peaceful
But is there a time for strength
Is there a time to stand firm and protect
To say no
To take up arms of righteousness
Against the darkness and those who carry it
I do not know
I get puffed up with rightness and see an enemy
But the enemy is always me
Teach me to be a warrior in your service
To be brave in waging obedience
To be yielding like the sapling rooted in the soil of
    your love, always green
Help me understand my place
I need you so much
I can't do this by myself
Please help me
Help me do what is right

Your discomfort is irrelevant
This is not about you
Your ego misleads you
None of this matters to me
We live together somewhere else
Come to me in prayer
Pray without ceasing
Nothing can hurt you
Nothing can hurt any of you
No battle except in yourself
    and not even there
Just an illusion
Breathe
Everything you need is in the breath
All is well

Goddess of compassion and grace
Help me keep my heart open in love
I feel frustrated and discouraged
With the choices a loved one makes
Help me live into her name
I feel at a loss, repelled, impatient
Wanting things to be different
Full of judgment and condemnation
Love is blocked by anger
What am I afraid of?
Guide me, lead me to surrender all to you
All problems are solved
Because there are no problems
We all rest in your eternal embrace
But....
Help me please

Life is suffering
As long as you live in this world
There will be separation and suffering
You see what you choose to see
Leave it all
Come to me with your whole self
Abide with me and in me
As I abide with you and in you
Come through the narrow gate of the Way
Come through and stay
   in trust
      and light
         and love

Lord of light and grace
I come to you again
With spirit churned and muddy
Full of judgment and frustration
An ego attacked and seeking to defend
Where does grace stop and enabling begin
I keep chewing on a conversation
Getting angrier and angrier
Rehearsing again and again what I want to say
All words carrying the same message
You are wrong and I am right
Lashing out in self righteousness
It is so appealing
I feel vindicated and powerful...
    and so wrong
        and so stuck
            and so aggrieved
I'm asking for help
I know I cannot do this of myself
I want only you
Please help me mean that
Break me free
Bring me home

The ego struggles child
If you do battle it will win
    or at least appear to
Battle is unknown to me
Do what is right
Leave the rest to me
Live with me at the beginning of heaven and earth
Rest in peace and joy
Nothing else is real
Thank your teachers
Bless all
For all are you
    in me
Go in peace

Wise one of clarity and truth
Shine your light on me
Show me your path
Guide my steps
Dreams, pains, inner callings, emotions, thoughts
All jumbling tumbling
Confusing
So loud
Something big I can't see
Something important I can't hear
I want to see and hear only you
Help me find your outstretched hand
Don't let me go
Giver of life and light and everything that is pure
    and true
Help me wake up to your love

Child of the universal covenant
You are never lost
I have never let you go
Smoke and mirrors are all you see
Stop looking with your eyes
And listening with your ears
See and hear with your heart
My song sings in your spirit
Think not
And you will know what to do
Go in peace beloved

Such sadness
Something moving, shifting
Pain—trying to break free
Disoriented
Unsure
Muddled muddied
Cotton in my brain
Thick
Wanting
Waiting
Watching
Testing
Alone
Thinking of my calling
A healer of generations
Remembering my childhood
Protecting those who should have been protecting me
I am close
At once eager and yet afraid

Big things, child
The veil is thin
Trust
Sink
Close your eyes and see
Here it is always
Come
Awake
You are close
You can smell it
Step
Silence
Now open

Lord of Light and Love
I seek only you
For you alone I wait
What wondrous miracles are laid before me
Like a feast for angels
I am blessed beyond belief
The veil thins more
Revealing the golden light all around
The air sparkles with joy
It is more than I can contain
So I choose to contain it no more
But to surrender myself completely
The shell cracks
And I am free

Joy rings in the heavens
Angels sing
Children dance
Beloved, O Beloved
Awaken from your sleep
I touch your eyes
Awake
You are home
You never left
Welcome

For you alone I wait in silence
Hear my prayer
Come to me and awaken me in your arms
Still the incessant noise
Open my mind to One Mind
Bring me home
I am ready
Give me faith to trust completely
Guide my every thought
Breathe my every breath
Let me not stray
Create in me a clean spirit
Wash away the dull and heavy muck I still hold onto
Help me let it go
Give me eyes that see only your light
Ears that hear only your song
And a heart that loves as you love
These things I ask

Child of my heart
Leave all your worries at my feet
They are nothing
Let them go
Rest
And I will carry you
Sink into my arms
Close your eyes
And dream of wonder
Pure and innocent
Full of light and laughter
Relinquish judgment
And enter the gates of paradise
In this holy instant
Now
That is all
There is nothing else
Come here to me
Awake!
I love thee so

Why would I ever choose to enter turbulence
Why would I leave the deep peace of your love
Why would I allow agitation to stir up my heart
Why would I attach my contentment to someone
    else's behavior
Why would I enter fear and interfere
I shake my head
I know better
Yet I do it
Ah this human business!
Please help me step back
Back into the light
    into the peace
        into the knowing
I lay all concerns at your feet
Confident that you hold us all in the palm of your
    hand
Ever safe and free

Child of my heart
This is not your job
Your only job is to love
From that love comes trust
Your efforts to control block the light
Release yourself and those you love
And even those you don't love
To me
My love is greater than all strife
Your love opens the door
Allowing angels to sail out
Covering all with their wings
Focus my child
On the only thing that matters
Let not your gaze be distracted
Be steadfast as I am steadfast
You will never lose your way
Remember who you are
Awake!

In silence beyond words
I come in gratitude for all the blessings of this year
A year of waiting
    for you
    on you
    in you
A waiting filled with tears and joy
    fear and courage
    releasing
    purifying
    purging
    falling away
Emptying what was stale and old and stagnant
Pricking what was stuck to let it all gush out
Clean and fresh and open
Thank you for healing and peace
Reconciliation and rebuilding
Gifts of grace
A warrior's spirit
Here I am
For you

Warrior child
The fire transforms and purifies as it gives light and
warmth
You have been faithful
You have trusted and followed
You have stayed awake at the watch
You have yielded and opened
You have stayed true
Come with me now
I have wonders to show you
We need no words
Take my hand
We'll fly
Come

In the dark mystery
Thank you for the glimpses
Help me go deeper still
I get excited and want to share
Guided or distracted?
We teach what we want to learn
But teach how?
The words are themselves distraction
Teaching becomes distraction
Yet wisdom guiding, guided me
Ah, circles
Teach me your ways
And guide me in the way you would have me go
Help me complete my way to you

Eager child
Delight of my heart
You will teach where you are
There is a time for that
But not yet
Stay and wait
Be still
Go deeper
I know it is hard
The razor's edge
Teach now the receiving
Return first yourself
Then reach your hand to others
You are your own student now
Teach yourself, my child
Teach yourself

One beyond all names
Is it time now?
A new book full and empty
A new group formless and eager
The wordless way seeks expression
Manifesting and returning
Prayer means two
Silence becomes one
Guide me
Be me
I give myself to you
To become you
So easy
Nearer than breath
Thank you
Thank you
Thank you

Beloved
The song of the universe
Vibrates in us all
Singing us into being
In the silence we return to nonbeing
It's so beautiful
So perfect
So perfect
I revel in it
So pure
So full of joy
Beyond it all
Within it all
Before the beginning
After the end
Creation
Spoken into silence
Returning
Be at peace

God of beginnings
I feel eager
   stirring
      restless
A jumble jammed at the starting gate
Ready to run an uncharted course
Or at least one unknown to me
Waiting for the bell to leap forward
To pour out when the floodgates open
To trust...at least a little
It's hard not to want to know
I seek signs and validation
Is this it?
Are you the one?
Is this the way?
Oh I wear myself out
Trying to figure out
The one thing that can never be figured out
The one thing that matters most of all
Until I surrender to the futility
...and there it is!
Until I reach for it
...and it's gone again

That moment of surrender is where I am
Always
In the dark emptiness that glows within
You cannot find your way here
Because it is not somewhere other than where you are
You cannot see it when you look
But only when you give up looking
You cannot keep it when you hold on
But only when you let it all go
Then it is yours forever
So close
The biggest step that anyone takes is the tiniest one
     of all
You will take it countless times
Until at last...no more
You are so close my daughter
Give up the struggle and rest in my arms
Like long ago
Yes, you remember
See?
Close your eyes and live

Dearest goddess of infinite mercy
What have you done to me?
There is patience
    where before l was hurried
There is compassion
    where before l was full of judgment
There is sadness
    where before l was angry
There is forgiveness
    where before l was punishing
There is understanding
    where before l was judgmental
There is welcome
    where before l was rejecting
There is joy
    where before l was miserable
There is peace
    where before l was in turmoil
There is faith
    where before l was afraid
How blessed are you
To shower me with moonbeams of miracles

Blessed are you my child
Full of faith
Resting in trust
Opening the door to let me in
How glorious is our love
We dance in stardust
This is how it was always meant to be

Lord of dark mystery
Shivers of delight shimmy through my soul
Where I am you are not
So I let myself fall away
And you are there
As always
Laughing to be found
Show me where I am
So that I may leave that place
To be with you
To be you
To be infinitely me

Child of my heart
I am found indeed
We play an endless game of joyous surprise
Waves lap the shore
Lovers in the moonlight
Darkness twinkles
Humming
Humming
Humming
Wonder all around

God of guidance
Leading through the dark
I see only an opaque wall
Something feels right
Yet something feels off
I try to figure it out before remembering
Oh right, I forgot to pray
So here I am
Trying to pray
While a part sits in the corner
Still trying secretly to figure it out
Hoping you will give me a crystal clear answer
So I will know instead of trust
Looking for the relief of certainty
While sensing that uncertainty is the lesson here
Trying to lead instead of letting you lead
Thank you for keeping me in the dark
Even when I'm not really grateful
Maybe especially then

Ah you do see
You see the mists of mystery
Truth in the cloud of unknowing
When you enter you are blind
And yet you know
When you step into the emptiness you leave everything
*   behind*
Yet you have everything you need
This is where we meet, you and I
Come sit in the darkness
Have some tea

What would you have me do
I thrill and quake
Fearing that what you ask will be too much
Yet wanting nothing so exquisitely but to do it

Write my book
Not with words
But with your heart
It will be revealed not by you
But through you
Stop wasting time
Stop thinking
Be still
And open
It will rise from the deepest deep
And flower

Lord of stillness and of movement
So much shifting!
People moving near and far
Relationships becoming closer and more distant
Trying directions then turning
This *is* your book, I think
The book of life
Writing itself bold
I'm listening

Deep listening
In the stillness
The center of all movement
Is the quiet source of all
No matter the swirling beauty
Creating
Destroying
Manifesting
Returning
In the dark
The quiet pulse
You listen well, beloved

Giver of abundant blessings
My cup overflows
It is never empty
Always pouring
Yet ever full
Blessings bubble up like a spring
And rain down like showers
Ones who have gone return with gifts
Angels visit disguised as old friends and even strangers
Moments break open and release eternity
Everything reveals perfection

It is the pleasure of all creation to sing giving
Blessed indeed are those who are open to receive
Listen in the stillness to the stillness
All of life sings there in one voice

I asked for a miracle
And then began to fear that I would get one
So predictable
Then the disappointment of realizing my mistake
Also predictable
So here I am
Coming hat in hand
To ask
Not for a miracle
But for willingness
True willingness
To receive what I have already
Instead of grasping at illusion
Wisdom teachings speak of effortlessness
Yet effort upon effort I make to not make effort
Around the circle once again
Help me in each holy instant to choose differently

Sweet one
Think not
Do not
Choose not
There is nothing to choose
Willing or not willing
There is only truth

Lord of truth
Source of all
I am vibrating
    humming
A joyous desire to share
To give as I receive
To teach what I want to learn
Hmm, or unlearn what can't be taught!
The words jumble and don't matter
Urgent excitement
Dancing peace
How
How
How

Stop!
Stop and allow
There is no how
Only opening
Opening and releasing
Releasing until there is space
Space for revelation
No effort
Just stop
Until you disappear
No fear my dear
No fear

Marvels of wonder and delight
I see
Letting go opens the way
No effort
Only allowing
Listening
Watching
Responding
Emptying my cup invites its filling
With miracles and marvels
Spilling over all
Sparkling waters of wonder
Starbursts bright
Lead me in the Way
I follow

It is easy indeed
Child of my heart
This is how it was always meant to be
How it always has been
And will be
There is no other way
I lead you in joy
We walk together always
Take my hand child
And awaken to your birth

Source of all
Source of me
I need help
I need you
Only you
A way seems clear
I take a step
It disappears
Two ways appear
Into the silence, delicious, alone with you
Or opening to manifest, invite, and share
Something so precious is happening
I feel it
And I fear to lose it
Excited and terrified
It is all I want
All I've ever wanted
To disappear into you
To awaken in your arms
At home forever

Rise up child
There are not two ways
But only one
The way of surrender
In silence or in sharing
Sink into me
Eyes only on me
Every breath releases
We give and receive in perfect union
Do not be distracted by choices that don't exist
Breathe into me
And die into the song of angels

Source of all and everything
That is what I want
All and everything of you
Help me mean that
With all my heart
I want to want you and nothing else
Help me release
What few remaining ropes of illusion I cling to
Help me let go
And fall into your arms
Help me walk into the fire
Knowing that only what I am not
Will be burned away
Leaving what was there all along
Me
Who is not me
But you
These final steps are not mine to take
But yours
Help me allow you to take them
Pour your mercy upon me
And bring me home

Beloved child
Beloved child
You already know
You make difficult what is easy
Your efforts choke
All that is asked of you is nothing
Nothing but everything
Your everything
Which has always been mine
What you hold onto is nothing
What you fear is nothing
There is no holding or fearing
You but play a game of illusion
Look again
The game is no longer there
It never was
Rise and walk away
With me

Great Oneness of the Universe
Thank you on this day of celebration of love
Thank you for my children
    and my children's children
Thank you for bringing family together
And for this perfect day
I am filled with humble gratitude
Thank you

A day like today
Is like a rock thrown in a pond
Ripples of love circle and expand
Until the world is filled with light and love
The heavens sing
And angels dance
Well done my daughter
Now rest and rejoice

Lord of time eternal
Will you teach me of time
Time is on my mind
As I sit here in stillness
After months of…so much
Families moving
Families grieving
Families separating and coming together
Reconnecting with old friends
Heart gifts given
Time speeding by
Now pausing
So many looking for more
Never having enough
Yet all is well
What can I understand of time

Dearest one
Is this a prayer of heart or mind
I know not of mind
In heart there is no time
What would you have me say
You will not find answers in mind's illusion
And in heart there are no questions
So be at peace my child

Ah child
You don't even know what your prayer is
It matters not
The answer is the same
If you are knowing
    let go of knowing
If you are seeking
    let go of seeking
If you are doing
    let go of doing
If you are trying
    let go of trying
If you are praying
    let go of praying
Let go of everything and listen
In the emptiness you will hear me
And know beyond your dreams

Goddess of patient wisdom
I hear
    and know
        and yet...
This bubbles up again
I turn it over and over
To find that way
That way of perfect seeing
So that I can be at peace
Final peace
Finally
The bubbles rise again
Filled with frustration and anger
No patience
No wisdom
No peace
Words fill my head rehearsing release
Sounding so well intentioned but not
Thinly veiling lashing rage
This is mine I know
I'm so tired of it
Please help me let it go

No no my child
It is not yours
Why do you make it so
You allow it so it is
You choose this
Why
You will not find what you seek
In the rage or words
Look deeper
Deeper still
Even more
Be still
And in the silence
Wait
Wait until the waiting ends
That is all

Giver of blessings abundant
Receive this day my humble thanks
Surrounded by food and warmth
Held in the love of family and friends
My cup indeed overflows
What contrast to the woman
Bundled up in the doorway
Alone in the cold cold night
As cars pass by unnoticing
My heart breaks with helpless love
A plate of food covers not my shame
I didn't even ask her name
You have given me so much
Please pour your blessings on all
And guide me on your path
To help

All are my children
Loved
And perfect in my sight
Your heart troubles
Will I ask too much
What is too much
To one who has so much
Do not think or plan
But listen
Listen to your heart
And do not be afraid
My heart is big enough
For all

Teacher of patient reminders and everlasting peace
I am distracted and disturbed by what I see
So much anger and fear
Voiced into the world
And acted upon
Separation and deadly posturing
Leading not to light
But cycling, circling
In a whirlpool to darkness
So I asked for miracles
And was led to remembering
Why do I ever look away
Fold me under your wings
Fill my vision with light
And my heart with compassion
Let me not stray ever from your peace
Help me give witness to truth
And not be overwhelmed
Help me wait always
Like the watchmen for the morning light

Child who lives ever in my heart
And nowhere else
You stray far afield
Looking upon what is not real
The lure of delusion is sometimes strong
It is no less unreal
Spend not a moment in its snare
But shake off what you know is fake
Why sorrow over dreams
The dream is ever of separation
It cannot be other
Because it is not of me
And therefore ever not
What is of me
Is ever one
And ever is
As are you
Beloved
This you know
And nothing else is so

Spirit of winter wonder
The new year opens pure
As the snow falling outside my window
No footprints yet disturb its peace
Quiet and still
It waits
As I wait
Listening for you
Fill me as you will
I follow willingly
In joy
And humble gratitude

Child of winter
Born in darkness
Listen well to silence
Hear the crystal singing of your soul
The song of home calls all to come
All movement is returning
Let it be

Wise one of guidance
I circle restless
Swaying back and forth
Trying to force clarity
I know better
Help me wait
I thought to pray for an answer
But now I think to pray for faith
What other preparation do I need than that

One choice is the empty cup
Yet you seek to fill it
No need to choose it
Just do it

> *Child child*
> *What upsets you so*
> *Give me your concerns*
> *What irks you so*
> *How important could it be*

I am ashamed, and it's easier to be angry with someone else than to admit how bad I feel, and how much
I regret choices I made. I can hardly bear to be re-
minded. I want to erase certain things from my life.
I feel like such a pathetic fraud. How can I bring this
to you? I don't want anyone to see.

> *Beloved*
> *I know it all and love you still*
> *Give me everything*
> *There is nothing that cannot be cleansed*
> *Human life is suffering*
> *But of this I know not*
> *You are holy*
> *And all this that torments you will fall away*

I don't understand. I am in this body and I set in
motion these things by my need and delusion. How
does it fall away when it keeps coming back?

> *It comes back because you still hide it. You suffer*

over things from a past no longer real. You suffer over dreams, dreams you think are real and cause you shame and anger. They are just stories. Let them go. What is your only job? To stay with me, looking only to me, nowhere else. Whatever distracts you, no matter how upsetting, is illusion. Anger and shame are not part of me. Only love. You don't need to do anything or fix anything or say anything. That is my *job.*

Thank you. I understand.

You're welcome

Giver of lessons and teaching and correcting

This issue recurs, always in the background, sometimes pushing to the front

Years before I pushed back in fear and anger

In recent years I've tried to stay open and compassionate

But also in some ways passive

Taking on blame that wasn't mine

Seeking resolution that eludes me

Blind to what others see

So now am I called upon to act

Or am I just seeking escape from discomfort and frustration

Am I waiting or avoiding

I can't tell

I try to figure it out instead of asking you

So here I am asking

Please guide me

Help me be patient and attentive

Or help me have clarity and courage

Whatever the path, your path

Help me follow it

Yes child
Seek me
You look to your own mind and heart instead of mine
The time to act is soon
But not yet
Stand ready
You will know
Stop rehearsing so that your heart will be receptive
Be like the watchman waiting for the morning light
Be like the warrior
    poised and alert
        calm and sure
Victory has already happened

Goddess of gentle wisdom
   and fierce grace
      and infinite blessings
Thank you for your patient guidance
   your marvelous kindness
      your soft corrections
         your endless miracles
Thank you for breathing me to life
In love

Child of my deep heart soul
So eager to be loved
Don't you know
You are *love*
Gloriously manifested
You are angel song
Humming in time and space eternally
Radiantly and ever perfect
Mine

Goddess of wondrous mercy
You have graced me with this precious gift
Your voice speaks to my soul
And my soul longs for you
Rejoices in your word
Delights in your love
So marvelous is this gift
It seems too much to hold to myself
So I share with some who also feel the mercy of
 your comfort
But I want nothing to distract me
Or to somehow muddy the pristine shower of your
 grace
Lead me in holding pure my desire only for you
Let me not veer from your gaze
Or be puffed up
Help me stay humbly grateful
And openly receptive
Without reservation or design

My child
It is a fine line you walk
The walk of pure faith
The razor's edge of trust
If your eyes are only on me
You will not trip or fall
Put your hand in mine
Close your eyes
And see with mine
Hear with your heart
The words I speak to your soul
The message is for you beloved
I speak to all just so
Encourage them to seek me as you do
And I will answer them
Entrust yourself to me
And pray in secret
Until I tell you otherwise
Share my love with the words I will give to you
Yield yourself to me completely
And all will be well

Lord of mercy and beneficence
My soul has sung these last few days
So full of tear sweet joy
Everything so precious
I see beauty everywhere
Thank you for giving me your sight
To see everyone as loved
We live in the garden
And know it not
Yet we are here with you
As always
And forever

Child of my heart
Beauty is yours
Is you
Love seeks itself
We smile into our own face
Through the mirror glass
So dear

So many voices
    crowding
    shouting
    whispering
    calling
Your voice is the only one I want to hear
Help me discern in the silence
Your voice and only yours
Like the sheep who hears the shepherd's call
Help me know your voice among the many
And follow only you

Precious lamb
I will not let you stray
Lately you have held a concept
Instead of listening
You look for something you think is special
Instead of waiting to receive the treasure trove
When you think you know what I will say
You hear nothing
Only noise
Humble yourself to wait
And in good time
You will see that what you want
Has always been yours

Goddess of infinite mercy and joy
Thank you for the deep peace and happiness
That well up in my spirit and overflow
Truly my cup runneth over
Forgive me for not expressing my thanks with every
     breath
Sometimes I'm aware of my blessing
But too hurried to do the one thing that matters
     above all else
What on earth (literally) could be more important
Than seeking your presence
To offer my gratitude for your inexhaustible bounty
Bless me with a humble spirit
With eyes only for you
And thoughts only of thanksgiving

You have been busy indeed
My beloved child
Returning outward to the world
There is a time for that
When your communion with me is so complete
It reflects the sun into the darkness
But if you get distracted
The light dims
And you forget again who you are
Remember first
Then share that memory with others
Take the hand of those reaching through the darkness
Your hand is mine when you remember
Go in peace sweet one
I am here

Wonder of infinite Oneness
You said there is a time for turning to the world
But is it now
My foundation in your spirit
Seems not strong enough
For all the things and thoughts
That pull my eyes away
Even in this quiet wonderland of beauty
I am lost in spinning tales
Instead of resting in your glory
My mind seems more chaotic than ever
And I fret over those I love
Instead of trusting you
I feed my ego with comparisons
And thoughts of specialness
Knowing I am trading true treasure
For glittering nothingness
Help me please turn only and completely to you
Trusting in your care
Surrendering in perfect patience for your direction

Dear one
Beloved
You come to me humbled
And knowing that you stray
That's all you need to do
I do the rest
When you ask for help
You are receptive to what is ever present
When thoughts arise
Don't judge or direct
But give them to me
Lay all your cares at my feet
And sing your way all day
Trusting me with every breath
I know your heart
All you love are with me always
Open yourself
And let love breathe

God of most infinite mercy
I am so sorry
How can I be so distracted by the ugliness I choose
    to see in the world
Instead of resting in the stillness of your joyous
    light and love
How can I be attached to an expectation that you
    will respond in a certain way
A way I have come to want
Instead of trusting that you will reveal what you will
When you will
In perfect harmony
[interrupted by phone call from a friend in need]
Thank you God for the call
For allowing me to see things in a different
    perspective
For showing me that indeed
We are all in the palm of your hand
And that all things do work together for good
Help me rest in watchful silence for you

I always answer you my child
Always
Our union is not limited in any way
The universe is our song of love

Goddess of infinite compassion
Who cradles hurting hearts in loving hands
Thank you for bringing me to this place
Of healing breezes whispering to my soul
Of green green bathing teary eyes
Of water teaching not to hold
All singing to release
And turn to you
Forgive me my distraction
It was nothing but a dream
A moment lost
Now eternity regained

You need never leave my presence child
Your willful jaunts mean nothing
Save to you
I am as close as your breath
Closer still
You suffer needlessly
Your heart is ever safe
With me
My child
Come here

God of mercy and tender comfort
I come to you again with hurting heart
So sad
So sad
Such grief awakened
Could an anticipated visit from so long ago
Stir up this pain
So sudden
From nowhere
I don't understand
My brain is thick
My body lethargic
Energy draining out
I feel like I'm sinking
I'm so tired
Please help me God
I need help
Where are my angels

Stop eating
    and moving
    and forcing
    and thinking
    and trying
    and struggling
Stop being afraid
What do you think will happen
Meditate on me
Breathe me
Watch
Wait
Let go
Sink
You will not drown
I promise
Wonders wait for you
In the deep
Wonders beyond your dreams
Do not be led astray
There is nothing for you there
Yours is here
With me
Trust me with your grief

I have gotten so scattered
I've let the rancor of the world creep in
I've let disrespect infiltrate my words
I've been careless with my thoughts
Help me stay focused only on you
With a yielding, open spirit
Ready to receive your guidance and blessings
Lift me up to shine your light into the darkness
Fill me with your unshakable peace
I'm so sorry for my mistakes
Create in me a clean spirit
Sharpen my attention
To watch and wait for you only and always

As day follows night
And the dawn always comes
So am I always here with you
As many times as you think you slip
I will call you back
To see that all is well
You hurt yourself with your posturing and distraction
But there is nothing I cannot heal
Because there is nothing really hurt
You live forever in the perfection of my creation
You live in beauty
You are forgiven every time you stray
Restored in your awareness of me
And who you really are
So come here child
Into my arms
You are forgiven by my love
You are forgiven always
Now let's go forth
Into this new day

What a busy year this has been
Each season bringing a gift yet drawing me away
I resisted then yielded
Not understanding but trusting in your purpose
Now I long to return to your quiet embrace
To spend time in contemplation
And prayer
And silence
Waiting and listening for you
What would you have me do

Just a taste beloved
Of returning from the mountain
Into the cacophony of this messy life on earth
People have lost their way
See with compassion
Pour the nectar of mercy on the desert of their pain
Let not the poison darken your soul
But transform it with perfect beauty
You can do this only by watching me
Look not to one side or the other
Eyes steadfastly on me
Until all else fades into shadow
This is your only job
Do it well beloved

One who takes care of everything
In infinite perfection
Today I am not seeing the perfection
I'm inserting myself in an effort to help
But am I?
"In quietness and trust shall be your strength"
Help me have a yielded heart
To be quiet so I can hear you
To trust in your perfection reflected in everything
I am focused on helping them
When all you ask is for me to keep my eyes on you
To rest and trust and yield

You see now that you try to direct one to not direct
    the other
For her happiness or yours
Does it matter?
You trust or you don't
You yield or you don't
Give them to me
They were never yours
You rest in returning
Let the current carry you
Carry you home
Float with eyes on me
Pay no mind to all the things passing by
One thing is no different from another
Let them be

Origin of time eternal, of all wisdom
Let this year not end without my understanding
    its lessons
A year unsettled
In my nation
In my family
In my spirit
Things emerging from the murky depths
Feelings
Fear
Unrest
Framed by friends and family visits
And one special from the past
Struggling again and again
To return to you
To remember you
To rest in you
Then distracted yet again
Help me understand
Help me hear you
And understand

Listen to the snow beloved
It tells you everything you want to know
The lesson of anything already past is that it's over
The snow erases tracks
All that has happened cannot be found
Everything is fresh and pure
A new beginning
Beautiful and full of promise
Sweet possibility
Look not back beloved
There is nothing there

Giver of abundant blessings
I am so blessed
Thank you for all the gifts you shower me with
How could anyone earn such riches
You give without regard to merit
The mind cannot fathom it
The heart cannot contain it
It overflows like a golden river
Thank you for blessing me
With a father's love
With my father's love
I feel him near at this time of thinness when he
    came to you
Such healing love humbles me
With gratitude so insufficient
Yet I give all I have to you

You are indeed a beloved child
Loved beyond time
By the father you know
And the one you can never know
Go in peace and joy

Bestower of blessings
Thank you for my life
I see you still have a few surprises for me
Whatever happens for the rest of my days
Please help me not fear
Help me stay focused on you
Please remind me that all is well
And to be grateful every day
Help me walk in faith
As I follow you home

Child of my heart
You reap your own rewards
Of faith and obedience
There is more than anyone knows
Out of the ashes flies the phoenix

Goddess of mercy
I have tried to follow you in obedience and joy
I am grateful for these years of walking with you
    in peace
But I know there were many years before that
Years of darkness
Years of wandering lost
I made so many mistakes
Some still bring shame
I want nothing between you and me
Please cleanse me of whatever remains unclean
Forgive me and restore me
Help me bring everything to you
So that I can walk with you
In perfect light and peace
And live with you forever

Child, you ask
And receive
Forgiveness is yours
Mercy is yours
Wholeness and joy and peace are yours
If you dwell in the past
You will be trapped there in illusion
Because it no longer exists
It haunts because you turn your attention to a dream
And make it real
Turn away and release it all
Turn towards me
And look nowhere else
Think nothing else
Abide with me and in me
You are home
Where you have never left
The dreams disappear in smoke
Let them go
Fear not the light
It is your home
With me forever

Wondrous teacher
Guide me please
With time the structure falls away
The steps merge and fade
What is there to teach
And how
I want to help
But I feel helpless
And so I come to you
Please teach your truth
And guide us all today

Dear child
You are learning faith
It isn't neatly packaged
It flows organic
>   *dynamic*
>   *whole*
Release the plans
>   *the thoughts*
>   *the structure*
Trust me
I know it's hard
This is your lesson today

Revealer of all truth
I hold a pearl
So perfect and beautiful
Simple and complete
How do I share it
I used to tell stories
Even Jesus told stories
Through millennia this is how we taught and
    learned
But what is the story here
Any effort to tell one
Seems to obscure the truth not reveal it
I don't understand
I don't know what to do
Please help me

The pearl is not for everyone
Your job is to light its way
Those who see will see
Those who don't will sense something passing by
Some will follow
Some will turn away
These are dark times in the world of illusion
Engaging with illusion makes it real
Stop thinking
Live the pearl
Be the pearl

After so long
Things seem to be rushing forward
I admit I'm a little scared
I want to do it right
I want to make a difference
I want to help
I want to empty myself
So that you can fill me up and spill over
Pouring your nectar of compassion onto all
    around me
I think to hang back
But I feel nudged to act
A sense of now is the time
Help me be the pearl

You have trusted up till now
Keep faith
This is your time
Open yourself
And let the light shine through
Light needs no direction
It acts of its own nature
Be light

Goddess of love
Help me
I am afraid
Something seeks expression
I am afraid to die
I don't know what will happen
I resist and want to stay
I want the peace and beauty
    but maybe the whole Truth is too much
I want it to be safe
    but it doesn't feel safe
And who are these others
I don't trust
Please help me

Oh child
You are ready
Give yourself to me
You are struggling to listen
Fear shouts in your ear
Do not heed
Listen underneath
By the cool pond
Prepare yourself
When the time comes
You will be ready
Let it go

Dreams dreams
Dreams of trying to get home
Not knowing the way
Or not able to get to transportation
Often about getting to the airport
But last time lost in tunnels and stairs and hallways
Then unable to find my car
Lord of home
These dreams—help me understand
Help me learn what these dreams teach
Help me get home

Are you sure you want the answer child
I know not fear
But something holds you back
And blocks your way
Fear is in your head
You try to find your way in your head
You battle fear and will not win
Cede the battlefield
Just leave
Remember when you realized
"I don't have to be here"
That is your lesson now
Come to me through mountain meadows
Along streams singing our song of love
I am where I've always been
As are you
Leave the dreams
They just confuse you
You need not find your way to where you already are

I don't feel ready
You say I will be when the time comes
But I feel inadequate
Scared and unprepared
Yet called—am I?
It seems too big for me
Please help me
If this is what you want me to do
Then please make it clear
And give me the strength of obedience
How do I get my puny ego out of the way
So that your glory can shine through

Let it be
You think my job is yours
Your mind darts here and there
Frantic
Leave your mind alone
I speak not there
You listen where I am not
And thus you do not hear
Leave your mind to its own essay
And come with me
Back to the garden
Have not a care
Why should you
Take my hand
And disappear into my arms
Why fear dreams
When you are glowing safe
Shining like the sun
In moonlight

I am ready
As you said
A teacher you made me
I did not know how to teach the truth
But now I know to trust you
It is your teaching, not mine
Help me empty myself
So that you can fill me with your light
To shine forth into the darkness
I yield to you in happy surrender
A great time is coming
I am excited
Thank you for all you have done for me
I am blessed beyond measure

Oh you please me so
Your surrender releases the power of heaven
The times are dark
Yet even a little light
Dispels the darkness
Follow me
And I will show you wonders you cannot know
Glorious is the light
That leads home

Lord of infinite wisdom
I didn't see this one coming
But I prayed this morning
And you answered
Not the answer I was hoping for
But I trust you completely
We are all in your loving hands
Keep them all held closely to your heart
Guide me in guiding them
Shine your light upon them
Pour your love over them
Thank you for answering my prayers
For your faithfulness unwavering
Thank you for blessings
No matter the form they take
Thank you for everything

Loved one
Answers are not always wanted
But when asked for are always given
What happened today
Was a miracle of faith
Trust that what you did was right
Guided by me to protect all
Look to me before you speak or act
Then you will know peace
Believe what you told them
Everything will be all right
Because it always is
You are loved
As are they
My ways are true
Know this in your heart
And trust in perfect faith

What a busy month
When prayers are answered
It is sometimes in big ways
So much happening
Shifts and changes
Light shining in darkness
Revelation
I feel a bit scattered
Revved up without clear direction
Contemplating humility while facing my own
    arrogance
Create in me a clean heart
    a humble spirit
        a surrendered soul
Help me turn to you first and always
And never turn away
Guide me this day and all days

Child child
Just breathe
Everything is in the breath
Love me
And my love will be freed
To flow through you
Everywhere
Bathing everyone in light and love
You struggle with the last resistance
The hardest
Release your grasp
And let the current carry you
It's so easy
Just let go
You are the light of my heart
Dear one

Source of liberty and freedom
What is the lesson you would have me learn
Am I holding onto something
Is something trying to release through my hands
This has been going on so long
It is moving towards the end
But it seems more active
Please help me understand
Thank you for this lesson

Control
Still control
Always control
Even this
What do you hold back from me
No need to know
But release it anyway
Just let it go
You are being purified
Let it happen

Goddess of love and heart
It feels like mine is breaking
What is this sadness flooding my heart
And spilling over
Why is something that is so much fun
At the same time so disconcerting
And upsetting
What am I grieving for
And how do I heal this pain
Please help me understand
What is happening to me

Love child little lamb
I am here to hold you in my arms
It hurts I know
But this release will set you free
You are afraid but trust me
I will not leave your side
Nothing is too big for my infinite embrace
Give everything to me
Hold nothing back
Do not hide in shame
Yield to me completely
I am sending you a gift
Do not tell a story
Open every moment
And receive my loving grace

Wonder of wonders
Something changed
    or shifted
        or transformed
          or opened
I don't even know what to call it
Everything exploded open
I am so filled with love
It cannot be contained
My whole being radiates and pulses ecstasy
Waves of holy passion rock my soul
I am lost in love
Release and liberation
I lay all at your feet
Thank you Lord of my heart
For blessing me so abundantly

Ah you see this glimpse of heaven
It is my good pleasure to give it
It has always been yours
Take it
Take all the love the angels sing
Let it lift you up
And fill you with light
You let all go
Now receive your rightful due
And live in my heart
Always

God of love and wisdom
How do I understand this
How do I live it
Heart spirit soars
Mind wants a picture
What does this look like
Head sees concerns
Cautions pay attention
I know
You said do not tell a story
Perhaps I know the answer
But I circle back
What does it look like
How do I live it

You do know the answer
Sit
Pray
Watch
Wait
Eyes on me
Trust
Breathe into the present
Every moment
My love is pouring into you
You cannot control it
Release your fear
What you concern yourself with doesn't matter
Step into the river
And be swept away with love

Holder of my heart
I wrote in such joy
But right after it was taken away
So quickly suddenly abruptly
I was too hurt and angry and embarrassed and
    confused
To pray
Of course that's exactly when I most need to pray
Now things feel more settled
But the feelings are still there
Reading the last prayers reminds me how happy
    I was
It was glorious
Then gone
Is such love really so fragile
So illusory
So transitory
Why can't it last

Nothing in this plane lasts, dear one
You know that
But the love that broke your heart open was and is real
Indeed it is the only thing that is
It is not meant to be laser focused
Then it only burns what it touches
It lives free
The liberated manifestation
The expression of my love
That brings creation into being
You cannot contain it
It will break out of any box
You have entered my realm
The only realm of truth
There is no pain here
You have been given a gift
Do not grasp it
Be it
That is all

Goddess of heart and love
I see now that while I thought I had surrendered
    myself to you
I hadn't
My heart I kept still safe
Safe in its detached coolness
But now I see
And I want to hold nothing back
I don't know how to love you
With that raw and complete abandon
Longing for you with every breath
With every heartbeat
I see now
That love is the way to you
Into your arms
Into your heart
Please help me learn the path with heart
The path of heart
I am here at your holy feet
Teach me

Your lessons have begun, dear one
No one comes into the bedchamber with an unbroken
  heart
The pain you feel is your awareness of love's call
You cannot be self-contained in my presence
You must dissolve in holy union
The doorway is through the heart
Trust me as you have in other ways
I will lead you step by step
You need not fear
Love beyond your possible understanding awaits you
Give your heart to me
I will not fail you

Lord of birth and death
Thank you for another year in this life
Thank you for continuing always to lead me home
Please help me not get stuck in the regret and shame
But help me see past and through all of that to you
Purify me with the fire of your grace
My head is so muddled
Love gets lost
Awaken me to your eternal embrace

You are where you have always been
Safe
Loved
With me
In me
Your mind will do what it will
Let it
Waste not your time on what is not
Love it
Love is where we are
Love is what we are
Give the pain to me
And do not fear it
What you call pain
Is just a thought
Look again
And see its beauty
Let it go

One of all knowing and all mercy
Beloved of my heart
What am I supposed to do with all this
What happened to wanting only you
To bursting open with love
To reveling in your presence
Now I can't even seem to pray
I am not full of love
I am angry and full of hurt
I can't even cry
So I write
But meanwhile I have lost the only thing that
matters
My connection with you
I am alone again
Never belonging
Please help me

Lamb child
My heart hurts with yours
Feel the betrayal and let it out
A child is so dependent
You were not protected
That is your earth experience
But I live not there
There is a different place
Not apart but bigger
Including and transcending your human experience
Broaden what you see
To include all and beyond
Feel what you feel
While never forgetting
That you are always in my arms
And in my heart
From that vantage point
All is ever well

I'm having a hard time with this
It hurts
Help me
The hurt is too big
I feel so small
I don't know how to deal with this
I don't know if I can

***

(later)
Thank you for my children
I am loved and cared for
I will get through this
With your help

Let your feelings out
They are big
But my love is bigger
I sent you help
You are loved

Warrior goddess of courage and mercy
Please have mercy on me
And give me courage to face my demons
I try to think my way through this
But I know that is not the way
I am lost and I do not know which way to go
Or what to do
I am still bound
Afraid of freedom
You promise that if we ask we will receive
So I am asking
I am asking for a miracle of release and awakening
I want nothing between you and me
I want to be fully surrendered to you
So please help me release whatever I still hold onto
    or avoid
Help me be brave enough to put my hand in yours
    and follow

Listen and wait, child
The miracle is yours
You hide what is deep
Do not look for it
Look at me
Only at me
Look at me and wait
What you hide will rise
If you look at it, it will sink again
If you keep your eyes on me
It will rise and be released
Do not believe your fears
Listen only for my voice
And trust that I will guide you through
You are safe and loved

Bestower of fierce grace
It rises up indeed
Loneliness
Loneliness that I remember from so long ago
Desperate for relief
Why have I isolated myself so much by my own
    choices
And now I feel so alone
Looking everywhere for escape
I have built myself a box
And now it feels like a prison
With an open door
That I'm too afraid to walk through
I forget to keep my eyes on you
Please help me

You asked and I promised
I give you this path out of love
You must trust me through your fear
Let the tears come
You will not be washed away
Give it all to me
A sacrifice of your whole self
All that you hold onto or keep secret
Give me everything
You will see
It will set you free
And you will soar
With angels in the heavens
Trust me with your life
And I will give you more than you can dream

Lord of this moment and of my heart
Help me open my heart fully to you
Right now
In this moment
Without reservation
Help me surrender to you completely
With my whole self
Surrender my whole self to you
Awaken within me a new vision
Your vision
Guide me every moment
In love

Child you are so close
You can feel it, can't you
My hand is here
Right here
Reaching out to you
You look again to earthly love
That is just a distraction for you
Trust me
Turn your eyes to me
Your longing is for me
Nothing else will ever be enough
I am your destiny
For this you are here
To reach across
And open the way
Just listen in your heart
I speak to you there

Lover of my longing heart
You are right
I do feel you close
In my youth I made boxes
Now I ask you to lift me out
To live with you
In perfect divine union
I long for you Beloved
My heart has awakened
The flame of yearning burns unquenched
The eternal flame of love for you
Take me into your sacred embrace
And never let me leave the marriage bed
I am for you
And yours forever

Yes Beloved
You are mine
We dance the sacred dance
Of eternal ecstasy
Life is our music
Give yourself to me in every moment
And have no other concern
Look not at what will pass away
But gaze into the eyes of immortality
And dance with me forever

Goddess of comfort and guidance
I want to hide away in the darkness of your robes
I am tired and ashamed
I feel lost and confused
I want to be held and hidden safe
I hurt
My heart weighs heavy
I cannot think or see
All is murky and muddled
Please help me
Hold me
Guide me
Protect me
Teach me in the way I should go

Child of mine beloved
Bring your weary heart to me
Lift your heart in joy at my smile
Let yourself release all care at my feet
You try to do too much
All is in my care
And will unfold according to my plan
You need not fret
Attend to your day
And I will attend to all
Be at peace
Trust yourself in me

I have made mistakes
I have caused harm
I am sorry—please forgive me
Help me do what I can to right the course going
    forward
My need was so great I could not see
Help me see now
Help me acknowledge my own failings so that I can
    heal that pain
In so doing I hope to provide support for others to
    heal theirs
Help me open myself to receive your cleansing love
To allow your healing love to fill me up
And pour out over all I touch
Thank you

My beloved child
You come to me in humility and willingness
That is all that is ever needed
I will guide you
Trust me
All that has happened has brought you here
Do not judge what is beyond your understanding
You ride the wings of angels
Who watch over you with love
And carry you on the winds of creation
Rest in faith
And watch the miracles unfold

Giver of mercy with infinite patience
I have not been praying
I don't know why
I feel like I have entered into a void of silence
Everything is so still
It's hard to move
So I don't
But at the same time I'm not waiting or listening
I am not attending
I feel scattered and unfocused
Sitting by the creek I wonder
What am I supposed to do
Activity seems to require too much effort
I am unmotivated to practice or learn
The world is whirling all around
While one day after another I do nothing
So I will pray and ask for guidance
Or just pray and not ask anything

You need not ask, beloved
I already know what is in your heart
Because your heart is mine
Your heart is me
Do one little thing
And then another
Your vision is too big
You cannot move
I will give you tasks
Small tasks
Listen and heed
Surrender to me
And all will be accomplished

Goddess of compassion and truth
Please help me now
Help me see
Help me see my own issues honestly
Help me speak and act with compassion
The usual question—what does that look like
Help me focus less on out there
And listen with an open heart to you
Help me stop trying to rationalize
    to escape
    to justify
Help me release my fear and let you move through
    me
To manifest your guidance and love for all
I am in a muddle
Please help me

Ah child
The muddle is always out there
Never in here
In here all is clear and light
You are in distress because you keep trying to control
You have an outcome in mind
And you strategize toward that
This is not your place
Keep your eyes on me
See your fear with love
You need your own compassion
Be a mirror
What is reflected is not your concern
Reflect what is real
That is all you can do
Pray without ceasing
Keep yourself open to me
I have all in my hands
Find peace
Be peace
Even in the storm

Lord of dark embracing
Night is here
At full tide
Spreading like a mist
Ere it ebbs before the light
This night of mystery
I come to you
With bowed heart
And humble spirit
Give me your blessing
In your overflowing mercy
Guide my steps
Where my eyes cannot see
Give me courage
To follow in faith where you lead
Fill me with the joy of your glory
Hold me close
And look upon me with love

Beloved daughter
You are mine
Come across the water
To my outstretched hand
Love me with the love I give to you
Behold the glory of your birth
You are blessed
My hand is on your heart
You are blessed
By fire purified
For heaven claimed
Listen to my words
And follow me
You will see
Wonders beyond all
This is my blessing
Doubt it not

Another year comes to a close
What a year
It feels like the lessons have sped up and gone deeper
Intense wave upon wave
Is this my life now—on the fast track
Will next year be like this one
One unexpected turn after another
Blessings, challenges, and surprises
A humbling year to be sure
Teaching me to trust
    to release
    to not interfere
    to surrender
Again and again
This is what I asked for, isn't it
To be closer to you
I asked you to teach me
    to guide me
    to purify me
A year of fire
I walked into the flame to you

Indeed my child
You asked
To the delight of my heart
My ways are not yours
You need not understand
Your willingness is everything
All that is required is your asking
Allowing me to give you your heart's desire
Everything you hold now seems so painful
Even a small thing
If it separates us
Feels like too much to bear
Continue to trust me
It will not be like this forever
You will hear my name in every breath
And walk with me in perfect joy
Surrender everything
And you will see
This new year will be full of wonders

Mother of mercy and abundant blessings
Thank you for this day of my birth
Thank you for my children and my grandchildren
Thank you for all the messages of love and caring
    and appreciation
Thank you for my health and my home
For all the abundance you have showered over my
    life
I am blessed beyond my wildest dreams
Thank you for my life on this beautiful planet
And for the love that you so generously fill me with
Keep me with you always
I could want no more than this

Beloved daughter
It is my pleasure to bless you so
You are my heart
Placed on the earth
To love and be loved
Enjoy this day with an open heart
To receive all the love coming your way
Bask in the joy of hearts giving and receiving
The bounty of love's existence
Open your arms to all the blessings
Falling like rain on all the earth
Today the portal is wide open
Step into the arms of angels
And dance
You are loved

Goddess of mercy
I keep holding on
At first I didn't think I knew what it was
But now I think I do
I am holding onto unforgiveness
To anger and hurt
And maybe I am still holding onto what is not mine
I need help
This seems too deep and too big
Do I think it's too big even for you
Am I truly willing to let it go
I don't even know
So I'm asking you for help
I'm asking for a miracle

Child beloved
You are not afraid of letting go
You are afraid of seeing what is there
The shadows growling in the dark
If they come into the light
You think they might tear you apart and eat you up
But what have you learned of fear
Do not obey
It is not real
Let it out
Lash yourself to me
And trust me through the storm
It will not last forever
And you will emerge light and free
Unburdened and unchained
And blazingly unafraid

God of gentle mercy
And fierce grace
I am here
Waiting for the tears
To wash me clean
Flush out all that remains hidden from you
Fill me with your radiance
Transform me with your love

You must wait
Impatient one
You are missing this moment
Looking for something that isn't real
You think you know
But you know nothing
There is nothing to know
Love knows nothing
Love is everything
What is there to know
So wait dear one
Wait with your whole self
For my revelation will come
But only in this moment

Mystery of transformation and revelation
What a hard time this has been
Ground shifting and falling away
Pain betrayal loss confusion
Grasping for something to hold on to
Peeling away the layers
Where are you
Please help me

This time is an answered prayer
Love leads you home
Love awakens you
Love reveals you
Cease your struggle
Beauty waits quietly
To be released
Manifested into all consciousness
What is peeled away is dense
Blood washes it away
Let it flow, flow freely
Go to the ocean
It is you

Lord of life and death
Everything is falling away
I'm losing everything
All my stories
All my perceptions
All my hopes and dreams
Everything I love
Everything I hold on to
Everything I know
Everything I think I am
Nothing is left
I am humbled in defeat
Brought low by my powerlessness
Emptied and stripped away
All I have is you
And maybe not even that
Just nothing

You have nothing
Because there is nothing to have
Form returns to formlessness
Desires stories hopes beliefs and dreams
All vanish in a blink
They were never real
The denseness you grab onto drags you down
You grab nothing
But the grabbing locks you into struggle
Remember your breath
It is the release that keeps you alive
The release into death
Again and again
Your agony is not unloved
It is love incarnate
Breathe the pain
Until you die into peace

I have not prayed
Held so tightly
I've forgotten how
Yet you have never left me
What is it that I can't let go of
And how do I release it
How do I call back to me
All those lost parts
I don't know where they are
Or how to embrace them back into me
Is my protector holding them at bay
Please help me open myself fully to you
Help me lay my body down
Swallow me up in your love
And make me whole in you

Child so dear
You are cherished in my heart
You need do nothing
Save allow
Allow me to heal you
Allow me to reveal you
You need ask me nothing
All is yours already
Love is yours
You were born not in human love
But in divine love
Let all these lost ones come home
Hand me the key
And it will be done
It already is

Giver of abundant blessings
I am awash in what I thought never to feel again
How blessed am I
By your loving grace
Full and rich is my life
Full of joy and rich with humble gratitude
You have done as you promised
You have carried me through the darkness
I kneel at your feet
And thank you

What else would I do
For one as loved as you
Why, no, how could you doubt
You would, no, could not
If you could see
How precious you are to me
Love breathes you
Love breathes your very bones
That breath is me
How could I not love you
With all of creation
You are ever mine
And ever me

You led me today on a path I did not see
My thought was for one thing I did not find
But there on the shelf was what I needed now
Thank you for correcting me
What are my gifts but little tricks
To make myself feel special
What could anything matter
If it takes my eyes away from your glory
You have called me to you
Let me not go astray
Let me not waste a moment out of your presence
Let me sit at your feet in adoration
Burned eternally with the flame of your love

Practice then my dear one
Practice with your whole self
Practice with every breath
Yes I have called you
But you must answer
In every moment give yourself to me
I am showing you the way
Follow me
And do not fear
For angels guard and guide your steps
You walk a sacred path
Into my very heart
You become my heartbeat
Feel it
When others listen they will hear
The heartbeat of the One

Here I am
Not sure what to ask
Not sure what to do
Not sure what to share with others
Not sure what to keep in my secret heart
Still stepping back and forth
Between the sacred and the mundane
Not sure of anything
I want everyone to know what I know
To experience what I experience
To be blessed as I am blessed
Guide me as you wish
Help me have the courage to follow

Again I say practice, dear one
All you ask for is already yours
Is already happening
You have become distracted
From your prayer and meditation
This is our time together
I am always here in this moment
You look for a plan
The plan is mine
You need not concern yourself with it
You will know everything you need to know
If you listen
Go in peace, sweet one

I pray to be released from the effects of any shame
    from my past
If there is any shame from times I felt humiliated
Please free me from that lingering darkness
Shine your light into all the shadowy corners
Sweep out the dust and cobwebs
Scrub me clean until I shine brightly with your love

I can clean only what you offer
So offer your whole self to me
Hold nothing back
It is not the shadows
It is the holding
That leaves you feeling so
There is nothing in the darkness but a dream
Made real only by your fear that it is so
Focus not on the darkness
But simply on your hand that blocks the light
Open your hand and see that there is nothing
Only the emptiness of a memory that is not real

One of destiny
I sense a shift
All the loosening of the recent years
Is now opening up possibility
There is loss and the pain of loss
I have been focused on looking back
At things I loved now gone
But now I see a glimmer of light
Beckoning me forward
Now it seems that all the releasing
Has been preparation for something new
This is what you have been asking me to trust
And just as you have always promised
You have not asked me to do anything
That you have not prepared me for
You have put something into my heart
A tiny seed
You are calling it to grow and blossom
I am ready

Hear me and follow
I prepare a way for you
Stay open and wait
You will know
Do not fear
Blessings await
You are my beloved daughter
Your faith has made you whole

Goddess of mercy and compassion
I hold such bitterness and blame
The walls are up
The doors locked tight
Please help me unblock your forgiveness
I feel stuck here
It is more than I can do without your help
So help me turn this over to you
For your healing love
Guide my thoughts
And lead me in the practice
That will set me free
I want nothing to hold me back from you

Come here my child
Such deep pain is profound
You seek to avoid it
But remember
Everything is a gift from me
The pain brings you to me
And thus is beautiful
Go into the pain and let it teach you
You will learn things there
To break you fully open
I am here with you
One breath
Then another
Listen
You will hear the song of my love
For this you have integrated
You are legion whole and strong
You are ready
And you are always loved

Answerer of prayers
You have emptied my cup
You have purged me body and soul
Of all impurities
I am here
Open and waiting
To be filled with your love
Until it spills out over the earth
Let nothing else enter
To sully what you have so thoroughly cleaned
Keep me safe in your embrace
Always in remembrance
Thank you for hearing my plea
And releasing me from the grip
Of what held me apart from you
I am renewed in your love
And want nothing else
But to remain in your presence
Forever

Dearest child
How can I not hear my own voice
When it calls to me from your heart
Purification you asked for
And received
It is my delight to give you what you seek
You need seek no more if you do not look away
Pray without ceasing
With every breath give thanks
With every thought give love
For this you have prepared
This is your high calling
In every moment
Answer

Lord of patience and endless forgiveness
Even after the precious gift of purification
I looked away again
How could anything seem so important
That I would tarnish or deny your love
Please help me choose differently
When I am tempted to turn away
Those thoughts and words do not reflect
The light that shines in me
I feel disappointed in myself
Help me pause before I choose wrongly
Help me see clearly the choice I am making
If I see clearly what I am giving up
For so foolish a momentary desire
I could never be so mistaken
Help me in every moment
With every thought and word and action
To listen and be guided by you

Child child
Go into the center
Leave it not
Practice without ceasing
When you stray
Come back
Your practice deepens and strengthens
Your desire to belong sinks you like a rock
You do belong
To ME
You lose your faith and falter on the water
Do not be afraid to shine like a beacon
They will follow
But you must lead
Look not back
Now is all
You are loved
So love, my dearest

Vast One of mysterious mercy
I am learning to trust
To trust completely
Practice always
Trust always
Listen always
Follow always
Love always
And in all ways
Thank you for blessing me
With one more day to love

One more day to love
And be loved
My darling one
You are precious in my sight
You have tasted the wonders that await
With each breath expand your heart with love
You need do nothing
The love is there
Just breathe it in and out
Do not doubt
You are my breath of love

Spirit of understanding and guidance
I am disturbed and confused by what I found
    yesterday
I don't know if it's important
Or if it sends a message good or bad
I don't know if or how you want me to respond
I don't want to mislead myself
So I bring this to you
Guide me as you will
Give me whatever understanding you wish me
    to have
Ease my heart back into your peace
I wait for you

Your words not mine dear one
Stories just stories
You give meaning to what has none
I say again
Follow me
Where doubt exists
I am not
Nothing need disturb your peace
I know nothing of disturbance or confusion
Here is only love
All else is a mistaken dream
Awake my child
You are ever safe at home

God of love and peace
Help me to choose only those today and every day
Help me hear your voice more clearly
Help me see with your vision more clearly
Help me love with your love more completely
Help me act according to your will more bravely
Let your thoughts be mine
Let your words be mine
Let your actions be mine
Help me choose you in every holy instant

Every instant you choose me
IS holy
Transformation is allowed
Allowing is practiced
Practice beloved
Practice with every breath
Until practice is no longer needed
Take no thought for the future
Just this moment
And this one
The gate to eternity

Holder of my whole self
I long for you with my entire being
Everything else falls away
My fear fades in the glow of courage you pour into me
You lift me up
And hold me in your embrace
Nothing else matters
Nothing else is real
Turn my eyes away from all illusion
Release my heart from grasping dreams
Keep my feet on the true path
Gird me with trust in your ways
Teach me to love as you love
As you are love
As am I

Beloved child
Your name is my home
I live in you
I am you
As you live in me
We are one
I hear your prayer
You ask for what is already and ever yours
Do not regret
One moment is eternity
Rest
And you will see

God of glory
You have clothed me in divine raiment
I am magnified in your loving mercy
You have stretched forth your hand
And I take it gladly
Leaving all else behind
I walk into your embrace
Shedding all density
I am robed in your splendor
I am yours now and forever
Blessed in bounty
Loved into eternity

Yes

Holy teacher
Let your words be mine
Let me speak what you would have me say
Help me surrender my thoughts to you
Help me trust that what needs to be said
Will be said
And nothing more
Thank you for leading me on this path
Help me honor you by word and thought and deed

You grow in glory
Reflecting the light from which you came
This is your test of faith
Your practice of trust
You need not know before it is time to know
Listen in silence
The words will come

Spirit of my life
Keep me safe from all that is not you
Protect me from the deluded creations of my mind
Burn from me every impurity
Allow nothing to enter my mind or heart or spirit
Except you, your loving fullness
Filling me up with your light of Truth
I ask for these things
These miracles of your holiness
Pour over me and into me
All that is you
Thank you for this year of expansion
    of integration
    of healing
Thank you for all my blessings
And for gifting me with faith
Your grace suffices me in every way
I am holy in you

Beloved
You do well to listen to me
Your faith deepens into the abyss
You are safe
Because you are one with me
Merged in the shallows
Rolling under
Now lifted to the stars in heaven
Perfect in surrender
Give all and you will see
That everything glows beauty
The beauty within you
Child
You are ever loved in my embrace
Peace be to your heart
Know it
You are loved

Beloved of my life and soul
I lay myself at your holy feet
I surrender my will to you
My thoughts to you
My words and actions to you
Take me into yourself
And use me as you will
Fill my mind with prayer
Fill my soul with humble obedience
Fill my heart with inexhaustible forgiveness
And boundless love
Give me a purpose
The wisdom to know it
And the courage to fulfill it
Purify my offering to you
And glorify creation
Lead me in your way
Now and always

You are not of your time
But you bring to this time
What I give to you
What I give to all through you
You have a warrior spirit
Embrace who you are
Stand ready
Watch for me
Wait for my command
You are my beloved right hand
You are well prepared
And equipped for what is to come
Let no doubt distract
Do not falter
Trust and have faith
All will be revealed
Know that you are precious to me
And loved beyond the heavens

Giver of this moment and every moment
Help me continue to release all that I hold onto
    from the past
Help me keep my attention on you
Only on you
And only right now
Thank you for everything that has brought me to
    this time
I bless it all and release it back to you
I need nothing but your guidance in this moment
To set my feet aright
Knowing that each step is placed in perfect harmony
With all that is
Help me live in peace
Trusting and faithful
With every breath

Rest assured, dear one
Comforted by words you recognize
Words that describe what you have experienced
These are my messages to you
Offered with love
Until you have no more need of them
You feel the weight now
Of something even as light as a feather
You are not afraid of what will happen
If you let it go and watch it float away
Then return your gaze to me
It was nothing
Just a dream that once seemed so important
With each release you shed the heaviness
The density dissolves
And we are here together
As we always have been
You are my beloved daughter
Welcome home

Goddess of mercy and forgiveness
Help me in my arrogance
My desire to be special
My love of praise
Even my desire to be humble is suspect
Tainted with wanting to be recognized for it
Honor and disgrace are linked to fear
Help me not be afraid
Why is it so hard to love you
    listen to you
    surrender to you
    follow you
When I know not just from faith
But also from the experiences you have blessed me
    with
That nothing compares to being one with you
Forgive me and have mercy on me
Strengthen me in you
Give me the heart of a lion
And the wisdom not to claim it

Child child
You look back at what was never yours
You have been led to a new place
One moment at a time
Look at me
Listen to me
You will have all
As you always have
And have now
Sink out of your thoughts
I am not there
Sink into the darkness
Where all is seen
I feel your struggle
It is holy
Persevere
Not in struggle but in surrender
Practice now
And now
All is perfect

Dearest child
I know you hurt
You hurt from the past
Seen now in the present
You falter in doubt
Here is my hand
You need not understand
Just take my hand
And walk beside me
In this moment is perfect peace
Breathe and listen
Rest in faith
Opportunities increase in love
See with my eyes
All is blessed

Embracer of union
What keeps me from you
Where do I resist
Holding on to what seems real
But is illusion
Pulled back into the mundane
Thinking it is important
Caught in a web of thinking
That matters not at all in the realm of Truth
I pray my prayer again
Whatever it takes
...and please help me mean it

Yes my child
Do you not feel my hand
I have your heart in my grasp
I crush it like a grape
The juice runs over my fingers
And drips on this world
Suffer all for me
Willingly
Unabashedly
Concern yourself not for aught else
Pure
Protect
You know this
Go deep
Abide there
In peace
Await

God of guidance
Holder of my heart
Leader of my soul
What would you have me do now
Everything seems so inadequate
Give me the wisdom of discernment
To know what you would have me do
Give me the courage not to hold back anything
    from you
Empty me out and fill me up with your holy self
Pour out through me—no, not me—
Pour out through this conduit emptied of me
Pour out yourself over this fevered world
I know from your gift to me that everything is
    perfect
Ground me in that trust unfailing

Darling one
This is the time
Your time
Take my hand
And walk across the water
Reveal truth
Do not fear
Be the lion's roar

Beloved of my soul
I am tired to death
I don't know what to do
Or what to think
Or how to help
Whatever seems to be
...is not
So much pain and suffering and fear
    and hatred and anger
It is too much to bear
Pleasure becomes illusion
Nothing is at peace
I am exhausted

Do you not know dear one
What is there to do or say
What hold you keep...on what
You think
You try
You live not where I am
You forget
And dream of what does not exist
Lay your burden down
Do you not trust me
That is what causes your suffering
Come here to me
Crawl into my arms and love
Receive me fully
Rest tonight
And wake up to a new day
Practice remembering
One breath at a time
It is enough

Galen Pearl is a writer, martial artist, and spiritual director. Author of *10 Steps to Finding Your Happy Place (and Staying There)*, and the blog *No Way Cafe*, her stories have also appeared in several *Chicken Soup for the Soul* anthologies. When she is not leading her Daoist contemplation group, practicing with her martial arts buddies, or playing with her grandchildren, you can usually find her sitting by the creek at her forest cabin in the mountains.

www.galenpearl.com

CPSIA information can be obtained
at www.ICGtesting.com
Printed in the USA
BVHW071340150322
631522BV00006B/190

Granter of mercy
I pray for him as I wish someone had prayed for me
I pray for comfort and faith
Knowing that he is in your hands
I pray for courage
To release my grasping efforts to control
I pray for peace
Trusting that all is as it is and perfect
I pray for perspective
Understanding that little things are just that—little
And not worth losing what matters most—you
I pray for humility
Realizing that I don't know...anything
Have mercy on me and teach me your ways
Show me the path I should follow
One step at a time